Millionaire Map

By Diana Bank

Diana Bank is not responsible for loss of capital and assumes no responsibility for the investor's course of action. Before deciding on any of the investment principles in this book, contact a financial advisor.

Any companies referenced in this book are not suggestions and used for examples only.

To my wonderful family, friends, teachers and coaches who helped shape my character and enrich my life.

AUTHOR'S NOTE

I was inspired to write this book when I saw how few countries in the world teach finance in their public education. Most people are left to their own devices to navigate the vast world of finance. I would like to provide a better alternative; a guide to help readers on their journey to a stable financial future.

It is never too early or late too learn about finance. In Singapore, children are taught the basics of saving and budgeting at an early age; financial education is integrated into the public school system. It's no wonder that it is currently one of the world leaders in finance, commerce and economics. Singapore also has the world's highest percentage of millionaires and is one of the least corrupt countries in the world.

The book will cover a wide range of topics to guide the readers on their financial journey. First and foremost, staying out of debt is paramount to anything else. When they learn the basics of saving, they will discover that compound interest is a gift that keeps on giving. It essentially earns interest on its interest. Financial planning can be fun and exciting, where how much money is saved and how it is spent reflects personal responsibility. Finally, they will learn the basics of investing their hard-earned money. This map is intended for anyone, from age 8 to 108.

Millionaire Map

TABLE OF CONTENTS

Author's Note **4**

Introduction **8**

Route 1 – Save Your Money **10**

Chapter 1 – Mental Money 11

Chapter 2 – Spending and Saving Habits 26

Route 2 – Invest **48**

Chapter 3 - How You Can Make Money with Your Money .. 49

Chapter 4 – Interest 54

Chapter 5 – Bonds 60

Chapter 6 – Invest for Success! 74

Chapter 7 – Mutual Funds 92

Route 3 – Retirement **96**

Chapter 8 - What is Retirement? 98

Chapter 9 - Types of Retirement Accounts 114

Chapter 10 - An Employer Plan 129

Chapter 11 – Setting up an Account 135

Worksheets **143**

Bibliography **151**

Glossary **153**

Introduction

You've already taken the first step by picking up this book. Now, all you have to do is follow the map. This book is your guide to becoming a millionaire.

In order for you to be a millionaire, you will need to learn a few key concepts.

This book is divided into 3 sections:

Route 1: Save Your Money

Route 2: Investing

Route 3: Retirement

In order for you to reach you destination, you will have to follow all the routes. You can't just pick one, each of them combined will help you become a millionaire. The best part is, that you can follow them all at the same time!

You will learn how to save money, how to invest it, and how to retire with more money than you would have thought possible.

Your
Journey Starts
Here

Route 1

Save Your Money

Chapter 1

Mental Money

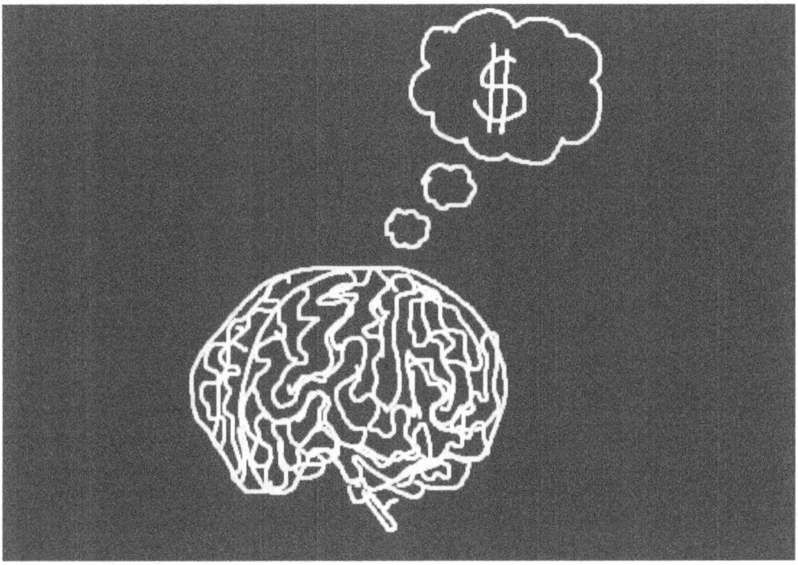

Not only do you have to learn how to save money, you have to learn how to spend it, wisely.

Often, when we spend money or purchase something, we behave irrationally. Behaving irrationally means not using good reasoning or judgment.

Dan Areily examines this irrational behavior in his book, *Predictably Irrational, The Hidden Forces That Shape Our Decisions*.

An example of irrational behavior in dealing with money happens when comparing the prices of two items. He gives the example of comparing two cups of coffee. One is $1.75 more than the other and comes from the expensive, better quality café. The other is less expensive and decent quality.

Judging rationally, we would examine the pros and cons of each, determine how that extra $1.75 can be spent elsewhere, and decide if the quality of the coffee is worth the extra money paid for it.

However, this kind of rational thinking would take too long in the real world. Instead, we rely on **heuristic behavior**, or what we did before when faced with the same decision. If we always bought the expensive coffee, we would buy the expensive coffee again, and vice-versa, even if rationally this might not be the best choice.

Understanding that we can behave irrationally can help us prevent doing so in the future by knowing what to expect. After sticking with one decision for so long, we can examine this choice and decide whether or not it was the best one to make.

THE POWER OF BRANDING

Saving right also means being a smart shopper. Many things we buy, we don’t really need. A good question to ask ourselves is, “Do I see myself using this 6 months from now? Am I getting my money’s worth when I buy something?” If not, we could probably do without that item.

The consumer marketplace is controlled by powerful, mega-rich companies who market their brands to consumers. A well-known brand doesn’t necessarily mean a good product. Sometimes, private label companies produce better quality products, but not always.

Companies are especially skilled in marketing their products so consumers will *want* to buy them. They put beloved TV show characters in advertisements. Children are attached to those characters and become in a sense, attached to the product. There is also product placement. Companies pay lots of money to have their product prominently displayed in a movie or game in hopes of attracting more customers to their brand. Advertising follows us from morning to night. It's there when we turn on the television, when we go online, and when we are at school. Corporations have succeeded in marketing to children and getting them to buy their product for a number of reasons. When we see famous people or our friends using it, we convince ourselves that it is cool. Famous people are often paid to promote certain products.

Being aware of different marketing strategies can save us from falling into their trap. We can shop for things and make smart choices without being influenced by advertising.

PAY YOURSELF FIRST

This age-old wisdom has a lot of truth, which David Bach goes into more detail in his book, *The Automatic Millionaire*. Every time you receive money, whether it is from your paycheck or allowance, pay yourself first.

For example: if you get $10 a week in allowance, pay yourself 10% of that money, or $1. Put that $1 away in savings before you pay off anybody else. This is a key concept, because if you don't pay yourself first, then you'll be stuck forever, paying off everybody else, except yourself.

THE HABITUAL FACTOR

In his book, David Bach examines what he calls "The Latte Factor". He describes the Latte Factor as an item that you regularly purchase, that although small, can eat into your money over time. Some people buy lattes, others buy candy bars, graphic novels, or a pack of gum. It doesn't matter what we buy, anything we regularly purchase is part of the Latte Factor. Let's take a look at the math.

If you get a candy bar every day or a similar low-priced item for $1.50, every day for a week, that is $10.50. After a month (approx. 30 days), that is $45, times 12 months (365 days) in a year adds up to $547.50. That is a lot of money! Here is a graph of the money spent each month for a year.

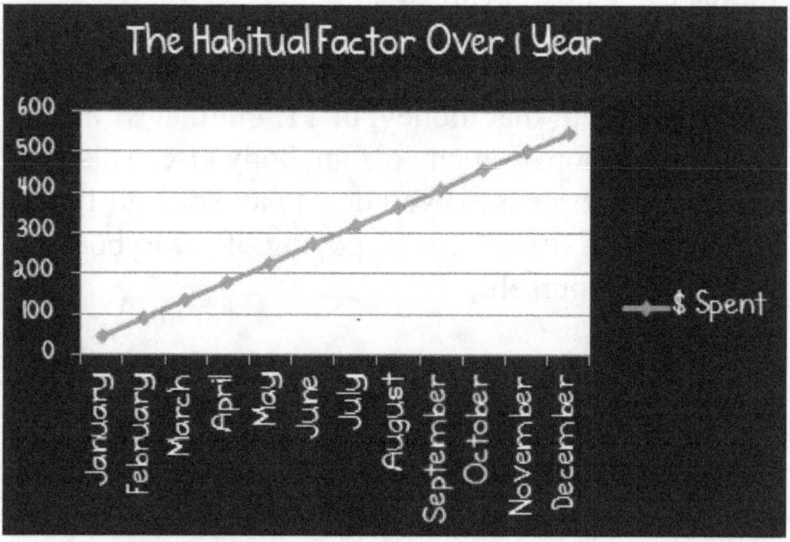

If you could save **$547.50** in just 1 year, imagine 5 years! It is the little things that matter, that over time, add up to large sums of money.

You can save money just by spending a little bit less on your Habitual Factor. Instead of buying a candy bar every day, you can buy it just a few times a month. You can still enjoy treats, but you are saving money too. Being smart about your spending choices can help maintain your financial health.

Try this exercise to find your Habitual Factor:

For a whole week, monitor what you purchase. Track your spending with the chart below and write down everything you buy for a whole week.

Find the day of the week on the left-hand side and put the name of the item that you bought next to "Item:" and the price of that item next to "Price". At the end of each day, add up all the items that you bought and put it under "$ SPENT DAILY". At the end of the week, add up all the numbers in the "$ SPENT DAILY" column and put the final result in the box next to "GRAND TOTAL".

Then you can see how much money you spent for the week and which items you habitually buy.

You will be surprised at how much the little items add up!

	ITEMS BOUGHT					$ SPENT DAILY
MON.	Item: Price:	Item: Price:	Item: Price:	Item: Price:	Item: Price:	
TUES.	Item: Price:	Item: Price:	Item: Price:	Item: Price:	Item: Price:	
WED.	Item: Price:	Item: Price:	Item: Price:	Item: Price:	Item: Price:	
THUR.	Item: Price:	Item: Price:	Item: Price:	Item: Price:	Item: Price:	
FRI.	Item: Price:	Item: Price:	Item: Price:	Item: Price:	Item: Price:	
SAT.	Item: Price:	Item: Price:	Item: Price:	Item: Price:	Item: Price:	
SUN.	Item: Price:	Item: Price:	Item: Price:	Item: Price:	Item: Price:	
GRAND TOTAL						

TERMINOLOGY

Interest - The charge for the privilege of borrowing money, typically expressed as an annual percentage rate.

When you put money into a retirement account or a savings account, the brokerage firm ("*n.* a financial institution that facilitates the buying and selling of financial securities between a buyer and a seller."), or bank will often pay you *interest* on the money.

Debt - An amount of money borrowed by person or group from another. A debt arrangement gives the borrowing party permission to borrow money under the condition that it is to be paid back at a later date, usually with interest.

risk - The chance that an investment's actual return will be different than expected. Risk includes the possibility of losing some or all of the original investment.

principal - The original amount invested, separate from earnings.

DEBT DESERT

Debt is one of the many obstacles on the road of becoming a millionaire. The answer is simple, *pay off your debts as quickly as you can.* When you borrow money, don't avoid paying off that debt. Debt can ruin a clean bank account like a worm can ruin a perfectly good apple.

Putting yourself in debt is like falling into a deep hole. Once you fall into the hole, *stop digging!* When you are in debt, don't borrow more money, pay off that money as soon as possible. It takes a lot of work to avoid falling into financial ruin.

Another important reason to pay off your debts is that the longer you have them, the harder they are to pay off. When you borrow money, you also have to pay that money back, *plus* interest.

Debt also goes hand in hand with credit cards. There is a big difference between debit cards and credit cards. Debit cards take the money straight out of your bank account the moment you make a purchase, so you are not borrowing any money. Credit cards borrow the money when you buy something. You will have to pay this money back within a grace period (usually 25 days). If you don't pay back the money in time, then the bank charges you high interest rates. This makes it harder and harder to pay off. The bank also allows you to pay the “minimum amount”. Paying only the minimum will keep you in debt even longer.

When you buy something on a credit card, you are creating automatic debt. If you have to use a credit card, pay it off within the grace period if you can. If not, then pay the debt as quickly as possible.

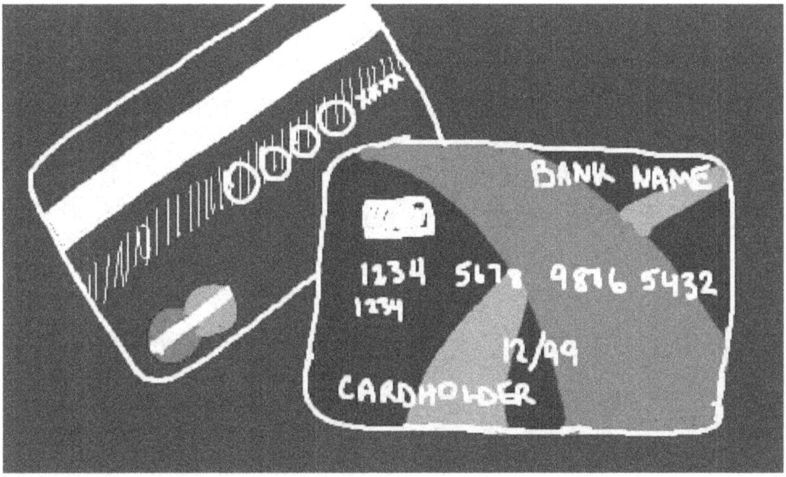

THE GIFT OF GIVING

When you do have a lot of money, it's important to share it with the less fortunate. Billionaire, Bill Gates has tons of money, yet he donates large amounts of it each year to charities. Why? Because he's helping various organizations and individuals live better lives, and he gets a sense of fulfillment. You can help in your own way, even if you're not a millionaire (yet). Donating even just $1 a month or your time for a good cause makes the world a better place.

Give, because it feels good, not because the Three Ghosts of Christmas are after you.

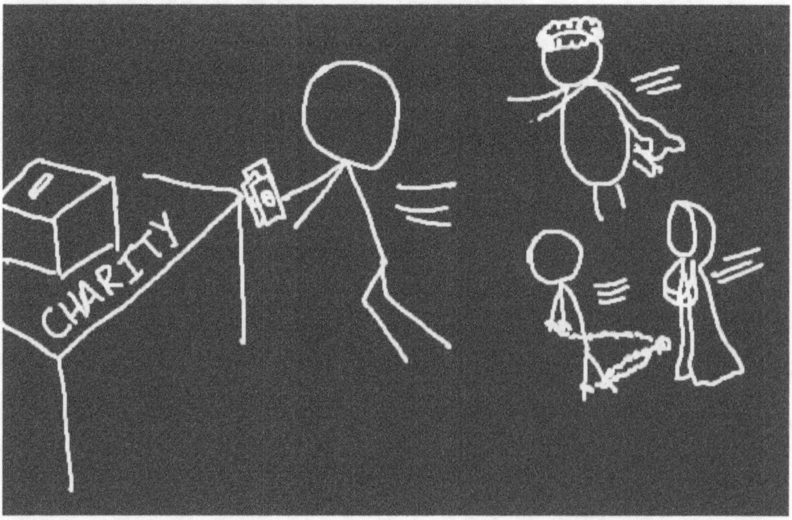

POP QUIZ

1. Should you put yourself in debt?
a. Yes!
b. No! Avoid it as much as possible!

2. What does Pay Yourself First mean?
a. Pay your brother for walking your dog
b. Pay yourself some money from your income before everyone else
c. Pay your bills
d. Pay for dog food

Answers: 1. B 2. B

Chapter 2

Spending and Saving Habits

The secret to being rich is not how much you make, but how much you *save.* Many people can make large amounts in income each year, but if they don't save a dime, it doesn't make a difference.

It's all about living *well below* what you can afford, not above. In *The Millionaire Next Door*, it explains how saving is the key to being wealthy. A little money saved now, can make a huge difference in the future.

People who make very little income each year, yet attempt to maintain high lifestyles find themselves unable to save properly, and are often swamped in massive debt. All because they are trying to live *above* their means, instead of below their means.

To live below your means, all you have to do is spend less than you make and save the rest. Then again, it can be hard to make smart spending choices and break bad spending habits. We are constantly bombarded by messages from advertisers telling us that we deserve better things in life and we'll feel happier, younger, prettier, and cooler if we buy their products.

One key to spending wisely is good common sense. Instead of buying something because it has a brand name, or because your friend got it, buy it because it's something you actually need. Not only that, be smart about your spending habits and buy it used or on sale instead of paying the full price.

Frugality is an important trait in saving well. Being frugal means not spending more than is necessary and only buying items that you need.

WANTS AND NEEDS

Being able to identify and separate needs from wants is the key to being a successful saver. Needs are things that you need, such as food, shelter, necessary equipment, insurance etc. Wants are things that are not a necessity, like games, junk food, toys, and so on. Frugality allows you to see your wants and needs and notice which one is more important to buy.

Being frugal means looking for things on sale and at discounted prices before automatically buying an item at the full price. It means saving your money and spending it wisely. It means being smart and separating wants from needs.

Some items may be both a want and a need depending on how you view them. A baseball bat may be a want to someone who only aims to play baseball recreationally, but it may be a need to someone who has a goal of becoming a professional baseball player.

Here is a list of some items that are wants and needs:

- A baseball bat
- Fruits and vegetables
- A car
- A new phone
- A video game console
- Paying for a doctor's appointment
- Gasoline for your car so you can drive to work

Practice separating the items into Wants and Needs in the chart below.

Wants	**Needs**

GOAL SETTING

Part of being a savvy saver is having goals. If there is an item that you want to buy, such as a new phone, or a video game, you can make it a goal that you work towards. For example, you want to buy a new phone that costs $200. You only make $20 in allowance each week, and you tend to spend at least $10 each week on food or going to the movies. That leaves you with $10 left over to put in saving towards buying the new phone.

$200 divided by $10 is 20. It would take you 20 weeks to save towards your new phone. However, if you were frugal, and decided to save all your money each week, it would only take you about 10 weeks to save enough money to buy the phone.

You can set both short-term and long-term goals. A short-term goal may be saving for a new comic book or a tennis racket. A long-term goal may be saving for college, or buying a car.

A goal should be measurable and it should have a deadline.

To quote Zig Ziglar in *How To Get What You Want*, "Do you want to be a wandering generality? Or a *meaningful, specific?"* Goals shouldn't be abstract, they should be specific.

For example:

“I want to buy a car,” is a good goal, but it isn’t written the best it could be.

We can change “I want to buy a car,” and add a deadline, and some measures. “I want to buy a car in 2 months, at an estimated cost of $4,000” is a better way to word this goal. It contains a clear objective, “I want to buy a car,” an estimated cost “$4,000” and a deadline to work towards “2 months.” You can make the goal even better and replace, “2 months” with a specific date, “May 1st” Finally, add how you plan to achieve that goal. By saving 20% of your paycheck each week? By working an extra job? Write down exactly how you plan to achieve it. Continuing with the car example, let’s assume you can achieve your goal by saving up some money each week. If you want to save enough in time for your deadline, you will have to put aside at least $500 each week. Congratulations! You now have a goal, an estimated cost, a method of achievement and a time limit.

Use this chart to set several short-term and long-term goals to work towards:

Goal Setting Chart:

Date	Goal	How You Will Achieve Your Goal	Estimated Cost	Deadline Date	Achieved (✓ or X)

THE MILLIONAIRE MENTALITY

There is a large difference between how rich people and poor people think. In *Secrets of the Millionaire Mind*, T. Eker outlines these differences. He says that rich people focus more on finding solutions instead of singling out all the problems.

T. Eker explains that your mental library is what determines the kind of thinking you will have. If you have negative files in your mental library, you will continue to think negatively about money. However, if you have positive files in your mental library, you will think positively about money. How you act depends on the files in your mental library.

Simply include files in your mental library that promote success. Rich people believe they are in charge of their lives. They take responsibility for what happens to them. They don't blame other people except themselves. They don't try to justify their situation, or act like a victim of their circumstances.

Awareness of what's in your mental library is only the first step. Next, you have to take action. Write down two things about your plans to create abundance. Put simply, net worth is all the debt you have from all the money you have. Write down your goals for net worth and income. Picture those goals in your mind every day as you work towards them.

Rich people think big and have large goals. Poor people are the opposite. If you don't think big, you can't expect to get big results.

Eker highlights the law of income. You are paid in direct proportion to the value you give to the workplace. The value you give at the workplace is based on several factors, including: supply, demand, quality, and quantity. Supply and demand is the number of products available versus the demand for those products. For example, if there is a new phone out, the store only has 10 phones on their shelf, but everyone wants the phone, the price will go up. However, if you have lots of phones (supply), but not enough people want them (demand), the price will go down. Quantity is how many people you affect with your product. How many people's lives are you improving or impacting? The larger the number, the larger your income.

Rich people see opportunities, potential growth, and focus on the reward. They take educated risks and research all their facts in order to make an informed decision.

Thoughts about your goals lead to feelings which lead to actions that generate results.

Those who are successful plan for the future, but live for today. They make reasonable, measurable goals and strive to reach them. Simply making the goal however, is not enough, you have to work towards it. As it says in *The Millionaire Next Door*, "I plan my work, and work my plan."

Actually working towards your goal requires courage and persistence. It also means deciding between instant or delayed gratification – "Do I watch a movie with my friends or work on my product idea?" Taking action is necessary to become successful. It requires spotting opportunities in the marketplace, acting on them, and profiting from it.

SMART SPENDING HABITS

In the book, *The Millionaire Next Door*, Thomas Stanley and William Danko explain how people have a hard time saving money from cash gifts. Instead of saving that money or investing it, they spend it, and often unwisely. This highlights a fundamental truth, it is much easier to spend other people's money than your own. However, you can't let this thinking get in the way of your saving.

When you get a substantial cash gift, don't spend it right away. Put in the bank. Leave it in your wallet for a few days. Resist the urge to buy something immediately. After a couple of days have passed, the immediate threat of wanting to buy something is weaker. If you still feel that the item you wanted to buy is a necessity, or something you'd like to have, go ahead and buy it. However, be smart about it. Try finding it on sale, or reduced prices, so hopefully you will still have some money left over to save.

PASSIVE INCOME

Passive income is making your money work for you, so you don't have to. If you can't generate a steady supply of passive income, you'll find yourself always living from paycheck to paycheck. Passive income can be generated in a number of ways.

You can earn passive income from investments or you can start and manage a business. If you create passive income from a business, it is only truly "passive" income if you don't have to be directly involved in the business for it to make money. This means selling a product instead of a service or being paid for your time. However, creating a stream of passive income requires time. Don't be afraid to plan for long-term gains instead of focusing on short-term losses.

Today, because of the internet, there have never been more opportunities to reach a global audience. You can create educational videos of something you have knowledge of and are willing to share. Then, you can put them up on Youtube and make money from the advertisements. You can also set up a website, write books, software, music, or sell artwork to create a stream of passive income. Essentially, you can make use of your talents to make some extra money that is not related to your paycheck.

INCREASING WEALTH

There are several ways to increase your wealth. You can work to earn a larger income. Which is important, however, if you increase your spending along with your income, you won't be better off than you were before. This leads to the next step. If you can't increase your income, or you simply want to save more money, you can simplify your life and live on less.

You can still enjoy yourself, while saving money. Put aside a certain percentage that you're willing to spend on whatever you want. For example, say you take 5% off the top of your income that can be spent on anything you want, such as going to the movies, buying a new phone, etc. You can't spend more than this. Limiting yourself to only using the money you set aside will help you save more.

You can also increase your wealth by getting educated. Learn about investments and take charge of your financial future. If you don't like your current situation, just know that you have the power to change it. You can start thinking in new ways which leads to new results.

BUDGETING

A budget is when you track the inflows and outflows of your money. You just write down every time you spend money and every time you get money. Budgeting is just making sure you don't spend more than you gain. You can see where the money comes from, and how you spend it. It allows you to track your spending habits and hopefully improve upon them. You can also "budget" how your hard-earned money is spent.

Budgeting is essentially a more detailed goal. Your goal? Spend less than you make and save money. How much you save is up to you, and what your financial situation calls for. Just remember, you have more control over your spending than you think.

First, you need to track the "Cash Inflow" or the money you take in. This can be money from a salary, allowance, or cash gifts.

Every time you get money, write it down in the "Cash Inflow Tracker" chart. Write the date you received the money, how much you received, and how you got the money. Keep a running total of all the cash you have.

Here is an example chart that tracks cash inflows:

Date	**Money From:**	**Amount**	**Running Total**
1/7/13	Salary per week	$500	$500
1/13/13	Extra work on weekend	$125	$625
1/14/13	Salary per week	$500	$1,125
1/17/13	Cash gift	$100	$1,225
1/20/13	Extra work on weekend	$125	$1,350
1/21/13	Salary per week	$500	$1,850
1/27/13	Extra work on weekend	$125	$1,925
1/28/13	Salary per week	$500	$2,475
1/31/13	Monthly income from Youtube advertisements	$56.75	$2,531.75

Below is a chart for you to fill out:

Cash Inflow Chart

Date	Money From:	Amount	Running Total

However, to truly create a detailed budget, you need a more detailed chart that tracks exactly where your money goes. Try this one for practice:

Home Spending:

	Monthly Cost
Home:	
- Mortgage / Rent	
- Home Equity Loan	
- Property tax	
Expenses (Utilities and Maintenance):	
- Gas and electric	
- Heating	
- Water	
- Phones	
- Cable / TV	
- Internet	
- Repairs / Upgrades	
- Gardner	
- Snow Removal	
Total Monthly Home Expenses:	

Food Spending:

	Monthly Cost:
- Groceries	
- Dining Out / Takeout	
- Coffee / Drinks	
Total Food Expenses:	

Car / Transportation Spending:

	Monthly Cost:
- Car Loan #1	
- Car Loan #2	
- Gas	
- Tolls / Paid Parking	
- Car Insurance (total all cars)	
- Public Transportation	
Total Car Costs	

Other Insurance:

	Monthly Cost:
- Health Insurance	
- Life Insurance	
- Disability Insurance	
- Long-Term-Care Insurance	
- Dental Insurance	
Total Other Insurance Costs	

Miscellaneous Spending:

Expenses:	Monthly Costs:
- Child Care	
- Private School Tuition	
- Entertainment (movies, DVD Rentals, Concerts, Sporting Events)	
- Hair / Manicures / Pedicures	
- Club Memberships	
- Computer Equipment and Games	
- Gifts	
- Vacations	
- Medical Copays and Out-of-Pocket Expenses	

WHAT TO DO WITH CASH GIFTS

Suze Orman says in "Action Plan" that when a child receives cash gifts, they should split it three ways. 10% of the money can be spent on whatever the child wants, such as toys, a video game, or a candy bar. 80% of the money will be saved for future expenses, such as a bike, or a new cellphone. The final 10% goes to a charity of the child's choice. This is to teach kindness and generosity towards others.

In the "Free to Spend 10%" column, list items that you want to use your spending money on and note the cost. In the "Saved 80%" column, put how much money will be set aside to be saved. Finally, in the "Charity 10%" column, put which charity you want your money to go to and how much you're going to give. At the bottom of the chart, log the total amount that you had as a cash gift.

Free to Spend 10%	Cost
Saved 80%	
Charity 10%	
Total:	

BUILDING A BACKUP

An 8 month saving plan is valuable wisdom that Suze Orman touts in her many books and on her show. She describes that an 8 month saving plan is a necessity in today's shifting economy. You don't know when you might be laid off or if your paycheck may be slow to arrive. Assuming that you'll always keep your job is a fool's errand. Companies are firing people left and right, not based on your valuable skills to the work place, but based on other factors, such as the out-sourcing of jobs, or tight funds.

Creating an 8 month savings plan means saving enough money to be able to support yourself for at least 8 months. Using the budgeting charts from earlier, track how much you spend each month and multiply it by 8. This is your baseline goal for saving up enough money.

8 months may seem like a long time, however it is necessary. You may need all those eight months, and more, to be able to find yourself a new job.

Building up an 8 month savings fund takes first priority over saving for retirement or college, but second priority after paying off credit card debt. Pay off that credit card debt as fast as you can, then focus on building a nest egg.

Route 2

Invest

Chapter 3

How You Can Make Money with Your Money

If you really think about it, keeping your money at home doesn't make sense. Most of the time, you're tempted to spend it on things that have prices that will keep going up, known as *inflation*.

Another unfortunate side effect of keeping your money at home is that the longer you hold on to your money, the less it is worth. A solution to that is storing your money in bonds, stocks, or mutual funds.

INTRODUCTION TO BONDS

When you buy a **bond**, you are letting a government or a company borrow your money.

Bond - any interest-bearing or discounted government or corporate security that obligates the issuer to pay the bondholder a specified sum of money, and to repay the principal amount of the loan at maturity.

The good thing about bonds is that you lend the money, get it back on a specific date, and get interest (a little extra money). The issuer pays you interest for being able to use your money.

INTRODUCTION TO STOCKS

Stocks are pieces (also called **shares**) of a company. When you buy a stock, you are considered a shareholder.

stock — ownership of a corporation represented by shares that are a claim on the corporation's earnings and assets.

When you sell a stock, the price might be higher which means that you would make a certain amount of money depending on how much the stock went up.

For example, if you bought a stock of Bob's Building Supplies for $20.00 on Monday, and on Tuesday, the stock went up 5%. You would have just earned $1.

However, you would have to sell the stock for the money to truly be yours.

That same process would apply if the stock went down. If you bought Bob's Building Supplies for $20 on Monday, and on Tuesday, the stock went down 5%, you would lose $1. Then again, you would have to sell the stock to truly lose that $1.

INTRODUCTION TO RISK

Stocks, bonds, or other investments are each associated with different amounts of **risk**. Generally, investments with higher interest rates are more risky because you don't have absolute confidence that that company or government will pay you back. Investments with lower interest rates have lower risk. Stocks have more risk than bonds because the money that you invested is 100% at risk. The company is *not* obligated to pay you your money back.

POP QUIZ

1. What is a bond?
a. Money loaned to a friend
b. Handcuffs
c. Money loaned to a government or corporation

2. What is interest?
a. Meeting someone on the street
b. The charge for the privilege of borrowing money
c. Yearly income

Answers: 1. C 2. B 3. A

Chapter 4

Interest

Interest, in very basic terms, is rent on money. When you put money in a bank, you make money when the bank pays you interest. Interest is an important concept to understand when dealing with money.

TWO OF A KIND

There are two different types of interest. One is simple interest, and the other is compound interest.

> **simple interest** – interest calculation based only on the original principle amount.

An example of simple interest is if you put $1000 in a bank, and the bank pays you 0.21% interest each year, at the end of one year you would have $1002.10 (the original $1000 + the 0.21% interest). The second year that you had your money in the bank, you would have $1004.20 (another 0.21% of $1000 added to $1002.10 = $1004.20). The third year, you would have $1006.30, and so on and so forth.

YEAR #	STARTING VALUE	MULTIPLIER	INTEREST EARNED	VALUE AT YEAR END
1	$1,000	0.21%	$2.10	$1,002.10
2	$1,000	0.21%	$2.10	$1,004.20
3	$1,000	0.21%	$2.10	$1,006.30
5	$1,000	0.21%	$2.10	$1,010.50
10	$1,000	0.21%	$2.10	$1,021.00
25	$1,000	0.21%	$2.10	$1,052.50
45	$1,000	0.21%	$2.10	$1,094.50

compound interest – interest earned on principal (original amount invested) plus interest that was earned earlier.

An example of compound interest is, if you put $1000 in a bank, and just like above, the bank pays you 0.21% interest each year, but it is compounded annually. After one year, you would have a total of $1002.10. The interest is calculated and added to the account yearly on the current interest, and so the small bits of interest affect the next year's calculation. Money compounded annually earns more than simple interest because the new total amount is used to calculate the interest instead of just using the original amount.

Money can be compound annually, semi-annually, monthly, or daily. This means that the interest is calculated annually, semi-annually, monthly, or daily. The shorter the period of time before the next interest calculation, the more money adds up over the long term.

Here is a chart of compound interest, compounded annually at 0.21%.

YEAR #	STARTING VALUE	MULTIPLIER	INTEREST EARNED	VALUE AT YEAR END
1	$1,000	0.21%	$2.10	$1,002.10
2	$1,002.10	0.21%	$2.10	$1004.20
3	$1,004.20	0.21%	$2.11	$1006.31
5	$1008.43	0.21%	$2.14	$1010.54
10	$1019.06	0.21%	$2.14	$1021.20
25	$1051.64	0.21%	$2.20	$1053.84
45	$1096.7	0.21%	$2.30	$1099.00

$1,099! That's how much you would end up with after 45 years of compounding your $1,000 at the national average rate of 0.21%. As you can see, simply putting your money in a bank won't allow it to grow very much at the current interest rates. When the interest rates are larger, such as 4%, the benefit of compound interest is more noticeable. Many people choose to invest their money in stocks, bonds or mutual funds instead. This money can *also* be compounded. If a stock, bond, or mutual fund, grows at 10% interest each year, and you reinvest the profit, that investment is compounded at 10% each year.

For example, if you purchased a 30-year bond for $1,000 and it gave you an annual interest rate of 4%, which you compounded, in 30 years, you would have a total sum of $2427.26. If you decided to use simple interest instead, you would have been left with $1,900.

You can make your money work for you with compound interest in a savings account, brokerage account, or in a retirement account. **Compound interest** is one of the keys to completing your journey.

Remember, compound interest can only work its magic if you use it over the long-term, so the earlier you start, the more money you'll make.

POP QUIZ

1. Match the correct word to this definition: **interest calculation based only on the original principal amount**
a. Simple interest
b. Compound interest

2. Match the correct word to this definition: **interest earned on principal plus interest that was earned earlier**
a. Simple interest
b. Compound interest

Answers: 1. A 2. B

Chapter 5

Bonds

When you buy a bond, you are letting the government or a company borrow your money for a specific period of time. This specific period of time is known as the **term**, or how long you can hold your bond. Once the term finishes, or your bond **matures**, you get your money back on the **maturity date**. The government or company that you lend your money to is known as an **issuer**. When your bond matures, the government or company pays your money back plus a little extra known as **interest**.

When you purchase a bond, you get a bond certificate. This bond certificate gives you information about the bond. **Face value**, also known as **par**, is the amount of money that you will get if you hold the bond all the way to the bond's maturity date. The **yield**, also known as the **coupon rate**, is the interest rate you are getting on the bond.

Here is an example scenario. Let's say that you buy a bond issued by the government. This bond has a maturity date of five years, meaning that in five years, your bond will mature and you'll get your money back. The annual interest rate for this bond is 3%. You buy a bond worth $1,000. In 5 years, you get your $1,000 back, plus the interest x 5 years. At 3% x 5 = 15%, the interest is calculated to be $150. You are left with a total sum of $1,150. Way to put your money to work!

To review, bonds have:

- A maturity date (April 10, 2040)
- Par ($1,150)
- The yield (3%)
- The term (30 years)
- Different issuers depending on what kind of bond you buy

TYPES OF BONDS

There are three main types of bonds: **corporate bonds**, **municipal bonds**, and **treasury bonds**. Corporate bonds are bonds issued by companies. Companies use the money that you paid for the bond in their company. At the end of the maturity date, they pay you back your money plus the interest. Municipal bonds are bonds given out by your local government like city, county, or state bonds. Finally, treasury bonds are issued by the Federal government.

CORPORATE BONDS

Corporate bond – debt instrument issued by a private corporation, as distinct from one issued by a government agency or a municipality.

Corporate bonds offer the following benefits:

- Higher interest rates than municipal bonds or Treasury bonds (along with higher risk)
- Varied choices of investments (you can buy bonds of companies in any sector. E.g. Energy, retail, oil, manufacturing, biotech etc.)
- Steady income: Most companies pay you interest on the money twice a year
- Liquidity: Corporate bonds can be sold any time before the maturity date
- Corporate bonds are bought in units of $1,000

MUNICIPAL BONDS

Municipal bonds are issued by the state, county, or city (local) government.

- Interest paid every 6 months
- Interest lower than corporate bonds (less risk)
- No federal income tax on money earned from municipal bonds

TREASURY BONDS

Treasury bonds are issued by the United States. People believe that treasury bonds have less risk than either municipal or corporate bonds because the United States has enough money to pay everyone back. At least, that's what everyone thinks. As of now, the United States has $17 TRILLION in debt. The safety of treasury bonds is now in jeopardy.

There are different types of treasury bonds based on the length of the term and other factors.

- Treasury Notes (a.k.a. T-notes) - are sold like regular municipal and corporate bonds. Interest is paid every 6 months. Treasury notes mature in 2, 3, 5, 7, or 10 years. You can buy one for as little as $100, and they can be bought in multiples of 100

- Treasury Bonds - are sold just like Treasury Notes. The only difference is that treasury bonds only have a term of 30 years.

- Treasury Inflation-Protected Securities (TIPS) - Remember when we discussed inflation at the beginning of the chapter? Well, you can imagine TIPS as your own personal bodyguard against inflation (free of charge!) TIPS adjust the interest you earn based on inflation. If inflation goes up, your interest rate goes up in respect to inflation. Don't worry, just because your interest is adjusted doesn't mean you won't get your interest payments every six months (The only thing subject to change is the interest, not the payments).

- Treasury Bills (T-bills) –The terms for these bonds are from as little as 4 weeks to up to a year. Instead of getting paid interest in units every 6 months, you simply pay less for par. When you sell the bond, you get the full par. The difference would be considered the interest. For example, if you bought a T-bill for $950 and sold it for

$1000, the $50 difference would be your interest (or 5.26%). T-Bills can be bought for as little as $100 and in multiples of $100.

- Savings Bonds – The term is currently 20 years (varies with the current interest rate) and the minimum amount to buy one is only $25. You will have to pay penalties if you redeem your savings bond before the maturity date.

SAVINGS BONDS

- Series EE US Savings Bonds – With the paper version of the bond, you buy it at half face value and when you redeem it, you receive full face value. Online, you pay full par, and when it reaches the maturity date, you also receive the interest that it earned. They can be bought in units of $50 up to $5000.
- Series I Bond – You pay full par and receive interest on the money when it matures. You buy the bond at a set interest rate. On top of this interest, there is another interest rate that changes based on inflation. You receive this interest every 6 months just like corporate and municipal bonds.

THE THREE MUSKETEERS

BOND RISK

People determine which bonds to buy based on their risk. More risky bonds may pay more interest, but you can't guarantee that you will get your money back. Here's a chart of how bonds are "graded". A higher grade means less risk, a lower grade means more risk. Moody's and Standard & Poor's (S&P) are well-known bond rating companies.

	MOODY'S	STANDARD & POOR'S
SUPER SAFE	Aaa	AAA
REALLY, REALLY SAFE	Aa1	AA+
	Aa2	AA
	Aa3	AA-
REALLY SAFE	A1	A+
	A2	A
	A3	A-
NOT VERY SAFE	Baa1	BBB+
	Baa2	BBB
	Baa3	BBB-
PRETTY RISKY	Ba1	BB+
	Ba2	BB
	Ba3	BB-
A LOT OF RISK	B1	B+
	B2	B
	B3	B-
VERY, VERY RISKY	Caa	CCC+
	--	CCC
	--	CCC-
IS, OR MAY BE, IN DEFAULT	Ca	--
	C	--
	--	D

BUYING BONDS

Treasury bonds and U.S. savings bonds can be bought through a bank, your regular broker or the government's website. Corporate and municipal bonds can be bought through your broker (but only if you know what you're doing), and more commonly, through a financial advisor.

Here is a chart to help you keep track of the bonds that you bought and some information about the bond:

	ISSUER	TYPE	MATURITY DATE	PAR	YIELD	TERM	RATING
1	City of Bondville	Municipal Bond	January 1, 2025	$1,000	2%	5 Yrs.	AA3/ AA-
2							
3							
4							
5							
6							
7							

POP QUIZ

1. What is the name of the bond where you loan your money to corporations?
a. Municipal Bond
b. Treasury Bond
c. Savings Bond
d. Corporate Bond

2. What kind of risk does a bond rated with A+ or A1 have?
a. SUPER SAFE
b. REALLY SAFE
c. VERY VERY RISKY
d. PRETTY RISKY

3. What kind of Treasury Bond has a term of 20 years?

a. T-Notes

b. Treasury Bonds

c. Savings Bonds

d. B + C

Answers: 1. D 2. B 3. D

Chapter 6

Invest For Success!

It's a busy day as the sun dawns on Wall Street. A new stock is trading on the New York Stock Exchange. The Nasdaq is up 20 points in early trading. Oil futures are down and so are all the stocks in the energy sector. The latest model car from the CoolCarCorporation was recalled for a brake problem and their stock tanked by 10%.

This is probably what you'll hear from stock market commenters on investment channels on television. Yep, just your typical day on Wall Street. A lot of what they say will sound like gibberish at first; it just takes some time to learn the language. Let's get started and learn how to invest for success!

PIECES OF THE PIE

Let's put this idea of "stock" into context. P. Pie Corporation just opened for business. They have a store, along with a manager and 10 employees. Business has been good. People love P. Pie's pies. However, P. Pie Corporation wants to open another store at a different location, but they need money.

The CEO decides to issue stock of their company. Worth is the level that something can be valued or rated. They determine their company's worth and divide it into 1,000 **shares**. A share is a piece of the company. Imagine taking a pie and cutting it into 8 equal pieces, each piece is one *share*. These shares are priced at $10 each. P. Pie's friends, Doug Doughnut, Pizza Pete, and Carly Cupcake buy shares of P. Pie Corporation. Other people also buy shares. All these shares, 1,000 of them, priced at $10 each, were bought, which, when multiplied, makes $10,000 for P. Pie Corporation. They used this money to buy some retail space for their store at the new location.

A couple of months later, their new store is making lots of money. More people want to buy P. Pie's shares, but there aren't enough to go around, so the shares are worth more. Now, they are selling for $22 a share.

This is an example of **supply** and **demand**. When you have a limited supply, and lots of demand, things become worth more and are more expensive.

All the original shareholders are happy because their shares went up 12 **points**, or $12. They decide to sell their shares. They bought them at $10, now they are $22. $22 - $10 = $12. That $12 is their **profit**, or how much extra money they made.

This is a small example of what stocks are like in real life. Most companies will have more than 10,000 shares. One important thing to remember is that, if the stock goes down, the company is NOT required to give you your money back. This is why stocks are considered more risky, because you don't have 100% confidence that your stock will go up.

P. Pie Corp. is an example of a **private company**. Its shares are traded **privately**. When a stock goes **public**, it can be traded by anybody on a stock exchange. This is known as the **IPO**, or **Initial Public Offering**, when a stock is trading publicly for the first time.

PRIVATE EYE

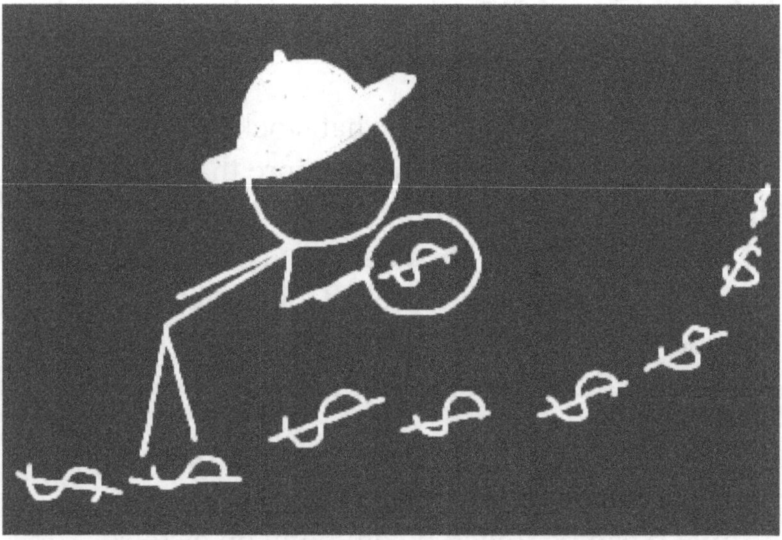

There are many well-known companies that are private. There are also many reasons why they are private. When you are a public company, you are required to release all your financial statements and make them available for anyone to see. When companies go public, their focus changes to the shareholder and that can affect how they operate.

There are many places in the world where stocks are traded. These are called **stock exchanges**. Some examples in the United States are the NYSE (New York Stock Exchange) and the NASDAQ (National

Association of Securities Dealers Automated Quotations).

When stocks trade on a stock exchange, they are given a **ticker symbol**. For example, Kellog's is K, Apple is AAPL, Nike is NKE. You can often check the price of a stock on a finance website by entering its ticker symbol.

The stock market and individual stocks are influenced by news, weather, trends, new discoveries, the general economy, and publicity.

For example, if a company called FindCancer Corp. suddenly discovered a new drug that helps prevent cancer, their stock would probably go up on the positive news.

If a car company had to recall many car models because they were badly engineered and the brakes wouldn't work, their stock would probably go down on the negative news.

Everything affects stocks, either positively or negatively. You can make money by predicting when good news will act positively for a stock.

Before you buy a stock, it helps to be well informed, or do your homework before hand. Like planning an attack, you don't want to rush into it unprepared.

Here is a checklist that will make sure you have a plan when you step onto the playing field:

1. FIND A COMPANY

- Listen to the news, read the newspaper and keep up with local events
- Notice new trends that are occurring, read the newspaper and keep up with local events

2. KNOW YOUR COMPANY

- You will often do your best when you know exactly what a company does.
- Find out on the company website, yahoofinance.com, or cnbc.com, how your company makes money.

3. DEBT

- Does your company have any debt? This is often a red flag that this company will not do well in the future. Keep in mind, that sometimes, companies do borrow money to expand their business. This is okay, as long as they can pay it off within the next year.
- You can look for a company's short term debt on their Balance Sheet, under Short/Current Long Term Debt.

4. P/E – Price to Earnings Ratio

- The price of the stock is not as important as it's multiple. The P/E ratio is the multiple. This is calculated by dividing the current price by the earnings per share (how much money a company earns divided by how many shares)

- In other words, the multiple (M) is Price (P) / Earnings (E)

- **M = P/E**

- You can compare companies by its multiple. A good rule of thumb is, the lower the multiple, the better the bargain, because you pay less for the price of the stock, but you get great earnings for the company.

5. COMPETITION

- The next step of your plan is to check out the competition

- If there are multiple companies in the same business, say, the automobile sector, you want to buy the company that has the most market share. If you want to buy a company, but it has better competitors, it will most likely be outdone by its better, bigger, competitor.

- It’s important to know your competition because you don’t want to be caught by surprise.
- Check out the competition by going to Yahoo Finance, typing in the stock quote, and on the left-hand side, you will see under Company, Competitors. There is a table with a few of the biggest competitors including private companies.

6. OPINION

- Before you buy a stock, it helps to be aware of what analysts think of your stock. Don’t always trust their judgment, but keep in mind that their actions can also affect the stock price.

Doing the homework is just making sure that you know your company very well. Watch the conference calls, read the news, and do the research on anything that may affect your stock.

To recap the HomeWork Checklist:

- Find A Company
- Know Your Company
- Debt
- P/E

- Competition
- Opinion

This chart can be used as a first step in researching a stock:

Sector	Stock	Symbol	Exchange	Price	Dividend	P/E
Food	Coca-Cola	KO	NYSE	$38.01	$1.12	19.68

In the first column, put the sector that the stock is in. In the second and third columns, put the stock name and ticker symbol, respectively. The Exchange is the market that the stock is traded on, for example, the Dow Industrial Average, or the S&P 500.

Put the stock's current price in the column labeled "Price" and the dividend in the column labeled “Dividend”. **Dividend** is extra free cash the company pays you for owning shares of their company. If you own 10 shares of P. Pie Corporation and their dividend is $1, you will get an extra $1 for every share you own, each year. This makes an extra $10 each year, which is free money!

Last, put the stock’s P/E ratio in the “P/E” column. This makes it easy to compare stocks and see their value.

The first row has been filled in as an example.

BUY & SELL

What determines the price of a stock? First, two terms to learn: the **bid** and the **ask**. The bid is the price that someone is willing to BUY the stock at. The ask is the price someone is willing to SELL the stock at. The price of a stock is determined when the buyer and the seller agree on a price. However, there are people all over the world who may be buying and selling a stock at a given moment, which is why you may see the price of a stock change many times in a given minute. Brokers are the ones who connect the trades between the buyers and the sellers.

You can imagine the price of a stock as a worldwide auction. There are bidders who BID prices to the sellers. The sellers ASK for a certain price and the bidders (buyers) BID a certain price. The one with the highest BID gets the sale.

ORDERS

You can buy and sell a stock in many different ways. The most common is the **Market Order.** This is where you simply buy and sell the stock at the current price, or the **market price**.

A **Limit Order**, is when you set a specific price that you want to buy or sell a stock at. An example is, if P. Pie's stock is trading at $20, but you think it is too high at that price, you can set a limit order to buy it as soon as it gets below $15.

If you want to sell P. Pie's stock at a higher price than it is right now, you can set a limit order to sell it once it reaches the price of $25.

There are many other different types of orders such as short, cover, and combinations of these orders, but these should only be used if you have experience in trading.

A **short** order, also called **short selling** is basically the opposite of a market order. In a market order you want to *buy low* and *sell high.* In a short order you want to *buy high* and *sell low*. You are essentially betting that the stock will go down, and when it goes down you make money. For example, if you short P. Pie's stock at $20, and you notice business isn't doing well, you are predicting they will go down. You *short* it at $20 (bought) and when they reach $10 you decide to **cover** your order (sell them).

Short selling is dangerous however because when you buy a stock normally, if the stock goes down all the way to $0, you'll only lose all your money, but you won't go into debt. If you *shorted* the stock, hoping they go down, but instead they went up, there is no limit on the highest price a stock can be, so not only will you lose all your money, you'll be in debt as well.

Stop orders are similar to limit orders in that you set a specific price you want your trade to be at. Once it reaches the point you specified, the stop order will turn into a limit order. Let's say you bought P. Pie's stock at $10 and the price goes up to $20. You want to hold onto them but you're worried that you'll lose all your profits if they go down. You decide to set a stop order at $15, this way, if the stock goes down and reaches $15, the stop order will turn into a market order and sell the stock at whatever price it is trading on the market then.

Stocks are traded in a brokerage account with brokerage firms. See Chapter 10 for a list of brokerage firms and their commissions.

EARNINGS

Every three months, or **quarter**, publicly traded companies are required to report their earnings, or how much money they had made during those three months. Their total earnings is divided by how many shares they own, so you get the **Earnings Per Share** or **EPS**. Analysts are people who predict the EPS of a company for the next quarter. If the company delivers lower than expected, its stock may go down and vice versa.

Part of doing the research is knowing when your company is expected to report. You do not want to be caught by surprise if your stock suddenly goes down 6% one day because it reported lower than expected earnings.

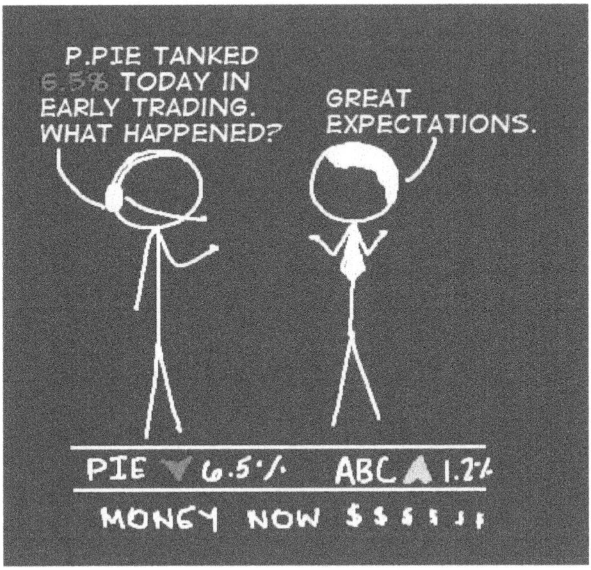

Use this handy chart to keep track of your stock holdings:

	Ticker Symbol	Action	Price	Number of Shares	Total Invested
1	XYZ	BUY	$25.00	100	$2,500
2					
3					
4					
5					
6					
7					
8					
9					

This chart can help you keep track of your portfolio:

Date	Balance	Investment	Cost	Money Received	New Balance
1/6/14	$1,000	Coca-Cola Stock	$500	$240	$1,240

Under the "Balance" column, put the current balance of your portfolio. In "Investment" describe what type of investment it was. The "Cost" is the money you spent on the investment. "Money Received" is the money you made. The "New Balance" is calculated using the "Cost" and "Money Received".

POP QUIZ

1. What is the ASK price of a stock?
a. The price someone is willing to SELL a stock at
b. The price someone is willing to BUY a stock at
c. To negotiate for cattle
d. To ASK a question

2. What is a Market Order?
a. Buying/selling a stock at the limit price
b. Buying/selling a stock at the highest price
c. Buying/selling a stock at the market price
d. Buying/selling a stock at the lowest price

3. Are companies required to be publicly traded companies?

a. Yes, definitely
b. No, of course not
c. Maybe.
d. Only in America

4. What is the equation that represents the P/E?
a. Money = Patience / Endurance
b. Monkeys = Plants / Eggs
c. Multiple = Price / Earnings

Answers: 1.A 2.C 3.B 4.C

Chapter 7

Mutual Funds

Trading stocks requires time and thought, if you don't have the time to do research, or don't want to, there's another route. Mutual funds. A mutual fund is a collection of stocks picked by a fund manager. Each year, the fund takes an average of 1.5% of your money to manage the costs of the fund. This is called the **expense ratio**. The expense ratio is the total money spent on maintaining the fund including everything from paying the fund manager to administrative costs. The expense ratio of mutual funds is rising over time. Exchange traded funds, or funds traded on an exchange, like the NASDAQ, typically have a lower expense ratio. These are called **ETFs** and can be bought and sold just like stocks. You can also use expense ratios as a factor in deciding which fund to put your money in.

There are many different types of funds, intended for different purposes and risks. Funds with fewer stocks and more bonds are less risky. Funds with more stocks and fewer bonds are more risky. Choose the one that is right for your situation. Some mutual funds can be purchased through a broker. Each brokerage firm offers different funds. Keep this in mind when deciding which brokerage firm to set up your account in.

Mutual funds are good for people who want to own many stocks, or don't have time to do the homework. Instead, all the research is done by a fund manager. Be sure to check your fund's performance and what securities it owns before going with that fund.

POP QUIZ

1. What is a mutual fund?
a. A peace treaty
b. Funds? Money?
c. A collection of securities traded by a fund manager
d. A traveling zoo

2. Who are mutual funds for?
a. People who don't have the time to research their own stocks
b. People who want to own many stocks and bonds at once
c. People who love the color purple
d. Both A + B

Answers: 1. C 2. D

Route 3

Retirement

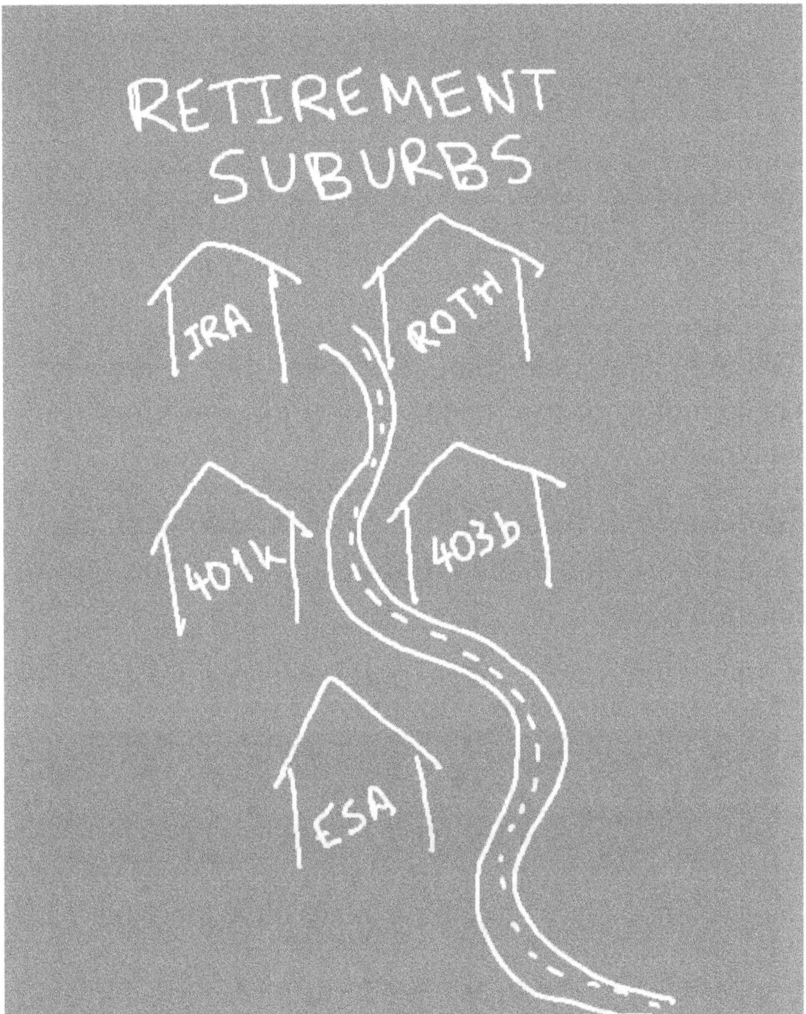
RETIREMENT SUBURBS
IRA
ROTH
401k
403b
ESA

Chapter 8

What is Retirement?

We will all get old someday (hopefully), and we will need money to live since we won't be working anymore.

Retirement is the term for when you stop working. Usually, people begin retirement between the ages of 60 and 65.

retirement - withdrawal from one's position or occupation or from active working life

The key to retiring rich is starting early. The earlier you start, the better off you'll be. If you started saving at age 15, you could be a millionaire by age 45 and retire early. Not to leave you wiser folks out, you can be millionaires too, but you will have to work harder. You will have to make up for time lost in your younger years.

Putting money away now lets compound interest work its magic, to have money saved when you're ready to retire.

INTRODUCTION TO RETIREMENT ACCOUNTS

A retirement account is a holding tank for the money that you saved.

Pension plans are retirement plans from a private company, a municipality, or other employer. Once you retire, they pay you a portion of your salary each year, or pension. Pension plans are no longer used by most large corporations in the United States, however, some employers continue to use them. Instead, most companies have 401(k) plans where you set aside money from your salary to invest in the retirement account. The money is ready for you when you retire.

What you do with the money in a retirement account is up to you. You can invest it into bonds, stocks, or mutual funds.

ANNUITIES

An annuity is a plan sold by financial institutions that pays you a steady stream of money during a desired period of time. It works like this:

- You buy an annuity, decide how much you want it to pay you in the future, and for how long
- Each month, you contribute a certain amount of money based on how much money you want to earn later
- These funds that you contribute are expected to grow over time and be managed by the financial institution
- Once you reach a certain age (for example, 70), the financial institution will pay you a certain amount each month for a fixed period of time (for example 20 years) or until your death or other agreement

Annuities are good if you want the security of a steady stream of income each month during your retirement.

REVERSE MORTGAGE
also known as
HOME EQUITY CONVERSION MORTGAGE (HECM)

A reverse mortgage is a possibility if you completely own your home and are over 62 years old. The bank loans you a fixed amount each month based on the value of your home and how old you are and accounting for interest. As you borrow money from the bank, they pay off the borrowed money by owning more of your house. Once you die, the bank owns your house and is free to sell it to pay for the loan.

A reverse mortgage is a way to earn a steady income each month by slowly selling your house back to the bank. An heir may own the home if they can pay back the amount that the bank paid you.

RETIREMENT ACCOUNT QUALIFICATIONS

Believe it or not, kids can have retirement accounts. However, there are some strings attached. You need to earn an income (this is known as **earned income**). Making money from investments doesn't count (called **unearned income**), neither does allowance.

Understanding what a retirement account is and distinguishing between different kinds of accounts doesn't require complicated problem solving or intense mathematical analysis. All you need is some basic arithmetic and an open mind. So please, bear with me over the next few chapters.

TAXES

When you earn an income, the federal government takes a part of what you earn in taxes, usually between 0% and 40%. The government taxes you at different rates depending on how much you make each year and whether you are single or married. This chart shows the different tax rates as of 2013:

TAX RATE	SINGLE	MARRIED JOINT FILING	MARRIED FILING SEPARATE	HEAD OF HOUSEHOLD
10%	$0 - $8,925	$0-$17,850	$0-$8,925	$0-$12,750
15%	$8,926-$36,250	$17,851-$72,500	$8,936-$36,250	$12,751-$48,600
25%	$36,251-$87,850	$72,501-$146,400	$36,251-$73,200	$48,601-$125,450
28%	$87,851-$183,250	$146,401-$223,050	$73,201-$111,525	$125,451-$203,150
33%	$183,251-$398,350	$223,051-$398,350	$111,526-$199,175	$203,151-$398,350
35%	$398,351-$400,000	$398,351-$450,000	$199,176-$225,000	$398,351-$425,000
39.6%	$400,000+	$450,000+	$225,000+	$425,000+

To qualify to be in the "SINGLE" column, you have to be unmarried or legally divorced on the last day of the year.

To apply for "MARRIED JOINT FILING", you have to be married by the last day of the year, i.e.

December 31rst. You and your significant other file your taxes on the same tax return.

"MARRIED FILING SEPARATE" is for people who are married, but file their taxes separately. This works best when the couple is in different tax brackets.

Finally, "HEAD OF HOUSEHOLD" means that you are not married by the last day of the year and you have cared for one or more "dependents" (people) for more than half a year. You also paid for at least half the costs to house one or more dependents.

In other words, if you are single and you made $100,000 a year, the tax rate would be 28%. You would have to pay $28,000 to the government and keep $72,000 for yourself.

It could be pictured like so:

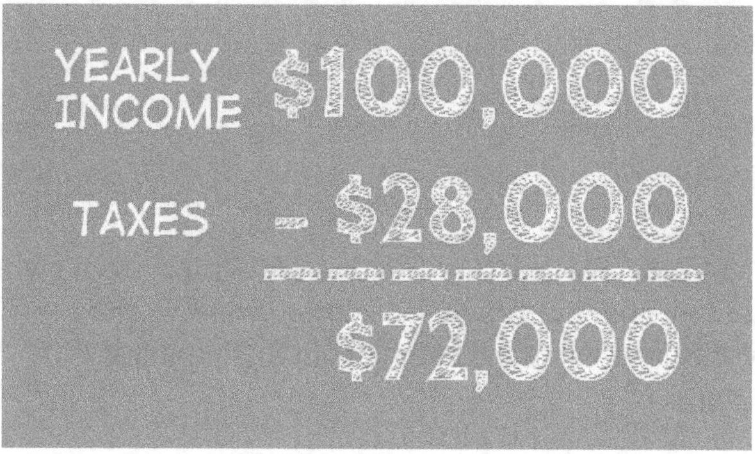

WHY DO YOU HAVE TO PAY TAXES?

Just like us, the United States has to pay bills. Where do they get their money? They get it from taxes. The taxes that we pay are used for, among other things, military defense to keep us safe, Social Security, and Medicare.

Social Security is a program that charges money to individuals under 65 through another tax on your income, and gives that money to people over 65. It's the government's way of helping the elderly. However, as of 2013, many people are retiring and living longer, using more of the money set aside for Social Security. The people who contribute to Social Security (everyone who is not retired) will probably not have that money available for their own use in the future. When the program was created, you could potentially live off of your Social Security payments until you died, but now the future of the program is uncertain.

Medicare is a government-funded health care program that helps provide health care for the elderly. There is a version called Medicaid that provides health care for low income families.

Here's a breakdown of exactly where your tax dollars went in 2012:

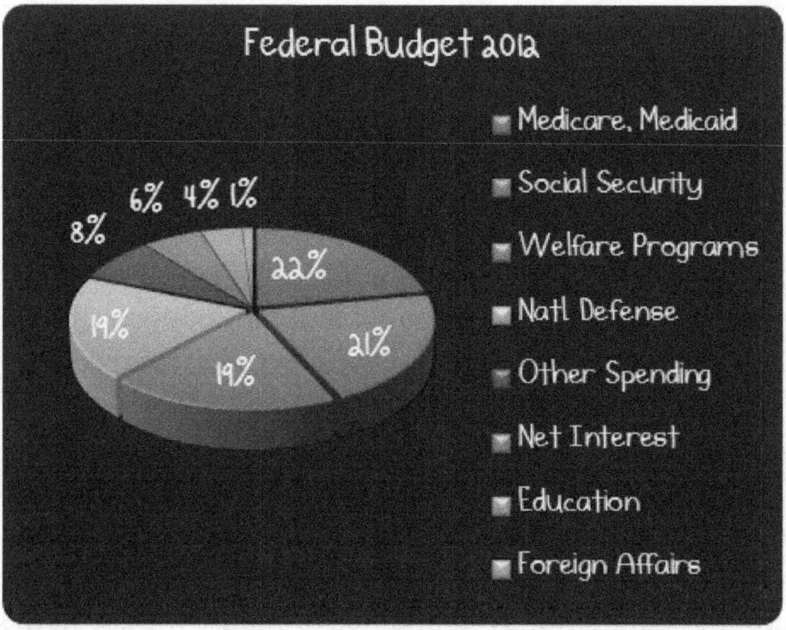

You not only have to pay income tax to the federal government, you also have to pay taxes to the state government. Every state except Alaska, Florida, Nevada, South Dakota, Texas, Washington and Wyoming require you to pay taxes. Instead of earning money from income tax, these states make money on other taxes, including property and sales tax.

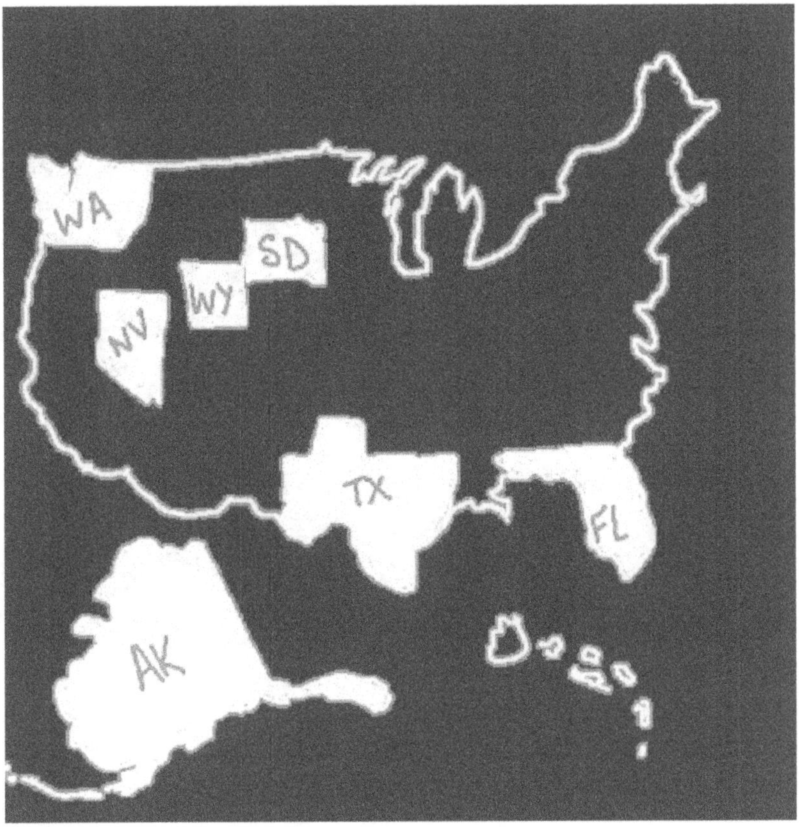

Most states have a scaled income tax based on your income and usually charge between 2 and 9%.

Below is the average state budget as of 2013:

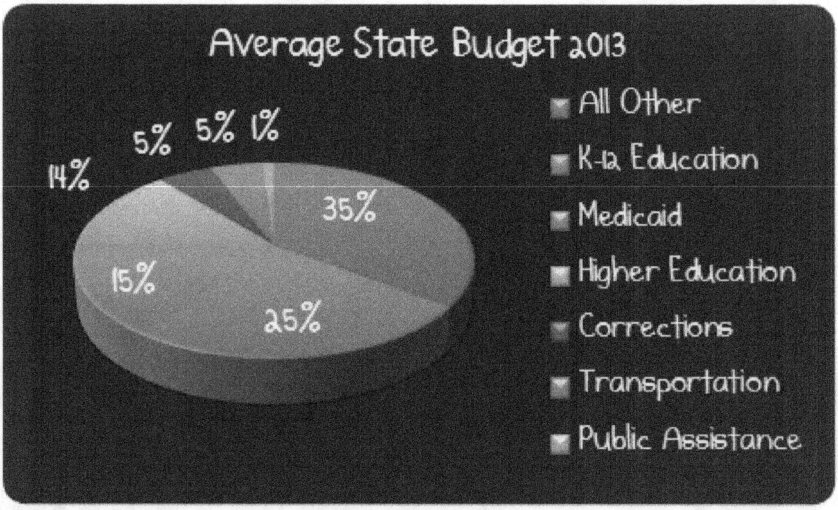

RETIREMENT AND TAXES

There are many different types of retirement accounts. Each one has different benefits. Many of the benefits involve taxes. The next chapter will explain in detail the different types of accounts.

One important benefit of most retirement accounts is that you can put aside money from your paycheck before you have to pay taxes to the government. If you wanted to put aside 10% of your income into a retirement account, you could put $10,000, which is 10% of $100,000.

If you put in money after taxes, you would have to calculate 10% of $72,000, ($100,000 - $28,000) which is $7,200. That's $2,800 less! When you put money into your retirement account matters a lot. Timing couldn't be more important.

POP QUIZ

1. What is a retirement account?
a. A box
b. A plan for saving money for retirement
c. Getting dentures

2. Do you have to pay federal taxes on your income every year?
a. Yes, everybody does
b. Only sometimes
c. Taxes, what taxes?
d. I only pay on leap years!

3. What is another name for investments?
a. Earned income

b. Money
c. Goldfish
d. Unearned income

4. Do you have to pay state taxes in Alaska?
a. Yep, everybody in the good ol' USA has to pay their respects to their state
b. No, Alaska is one of the 7 states that doesn't have state income tax

5. Would you be able to put aside more money into retirement if you got the money before or after taxes?
a. After
b. Timing doesn't matter
c. Before, definitely before

Answers: 1.B 2.A 3.D 4.B 5.C

Chapter 9

Types of Retirement Accounts

There are many different types of retirement accounts. The first is the IRA.

VOCAB LIST

IRA – Individual Retirement Account

In the IRA category there are several different accounts with various benefits. Here are three of the most commonly used accounts:

- Traditional IRA
- ROTH IRA
- Education IRA

TRADITIONAL IRA

A Traditional IRA is an account that individuals can contribute to each year. The money is held in this account until you retire. What a traditional IRA offers is outlined below:

- Tax Deductible
- No penalty if you withdraw (take out) money early for "qualified higher education" expenses
- Required to withdraw money by age 70 ½
- Maximum yearly contribution is $5,500 (as of 2013), or $6,500 if you're over 50

What tax deductible means is that the money deposited, or put into the account isn't taxed. If you earn $100,000 a year, and you put $10,000 aside into your traditional IRA, then the government only taxes the remaining $90,000.

Instead of paying taxes right away on the money in your IRA, you pay when you withdraw your money (usually after age 59 ½).

If you're under 18, you can have a retirement account too. All you need to do is earn a regular yearly income.

If you are a minor, you are not really responsible for the money, your parents are. Once you turn 18, the money is fully yours.

A WORD ON PENALTIES

In most types of retirement accounts, you can only withdraw your money after a certain age (59 ½). If you take your money out of the account before you turn 59 ½, then you will have to pay a penalty on the money (and taxes). The penalty is usually 10%. The government has this law in place to make sure that you only use the money for your retirement.

ROTH IRA

A ROTH IRA is a cousin of the traditional IRA, but there are some key differences:

- Not Tax-Deductible
- No Penalty
- NOT required to withdraw money by age 70 ½
- Maximum yearly contribution is $5,500 (as of 2013), or $6,500 if you're over 50

When you put money aside into your ROTH IRA, your whole income is taxed, but you don't have to pay taxes when you take your money out. It works like this:

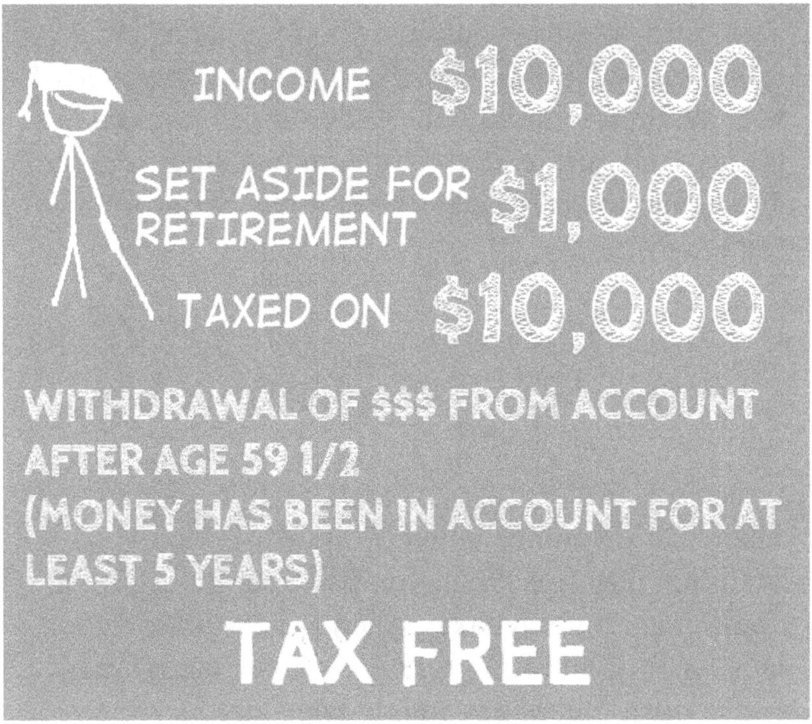

FACT CHECK

The ROTH IRA was named after its legislative sponsor, *William V. Roth Jr.*, a republican senator from Delaware. It was created in 1998.

You can withdraw your contributions at any time from your ROTH IRA tax penalty free. However, you can only withdraw the extra money you made in the account, also called your earnings, after you turn 59 1/2 and the money has been in the account for at least 5 years.

THE CONTRAST IS BLINDING

The main difference between the ROTH and Traditional IRA is when you pay your taxes. In the traditional, you pay taxes when you withdraw your money. With the ROTH IRA, you pay taxes when you deposit the money into the account.

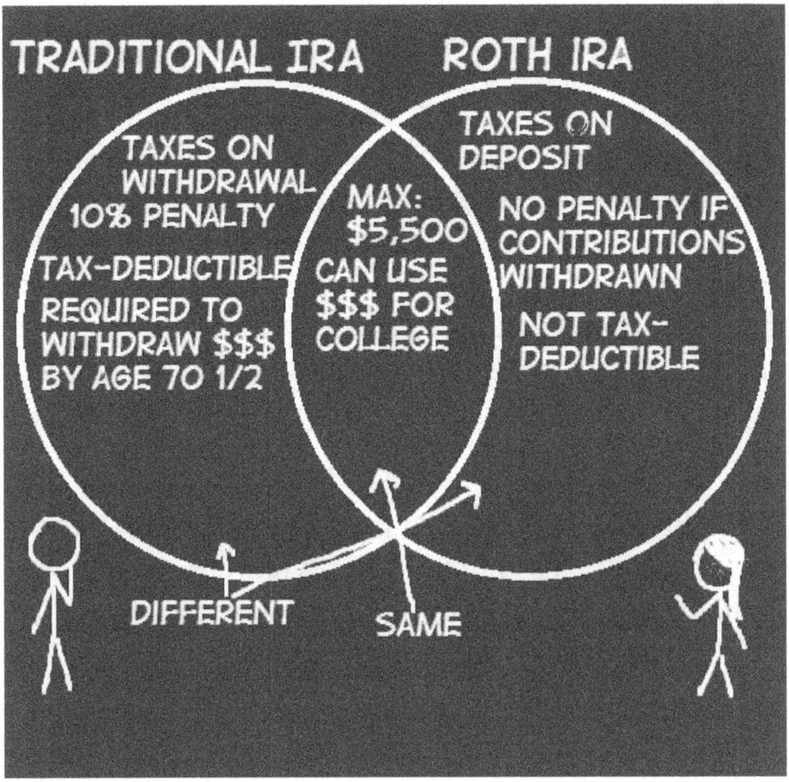
TRADITIONAL IRA
ROTH IRA
TAXES ON WITHDRAWAL
10% PENALTY
TAX-DEDUCTIBLE
REQUIRED TO WITHDRAW $$$ BY AGE 70 1/2
MAX: $5,500
CAN USE $$$ FOR COLLEGE
TAXES ON DEPOSIT
NO PENALTY IF CONTRIBUTIONS WITHDRAWN
NOT TAX-DEDUCTIBLE
DIFFERENT
SAME

DECISIONS, DECISIONS…

Which account to choose can be a difficult decision. The Traditional IRA is beneficial, for several reasons. When you put money into a traditional IRA, it's tax-deductible, saving you some money up front. Also, the more money you have in the beginning can generate more money with compound interest and earnings. Over a long period of time, this amount can add up.

A Traditional IRA is good for when you think that you will make less money when you retire than you do now. You can save on taxes now when you are in a higher tax bracket, and pay them later when you are in a lower tax bracket.

The opposite holds true for the ROTH IRA. If you think that you will make more money when you retire than you do now, you can save some money with the ROTH IRA. You can pay taxes while you are in a lower tax bracket now and avoid paying higher taxes later.

Choose which one works best for your financial situation.

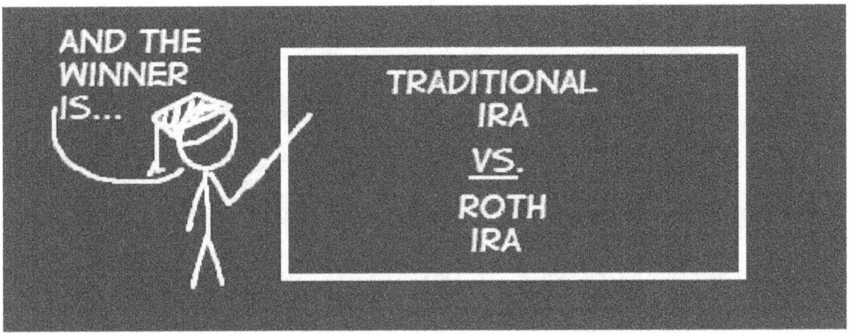

ESA

An ESA or Coverdell Education Savings Account is a special type of IRA.

- Money that goes into this account can only be used to pay for college.
- Parents are in charge of the money and they contribute to the account
- Not Tax-Deductible
- Withdraw money tax-free when used to pay for education
- Maximum yearly contribution: $2,000
- Money must be withdrawn before you turn 30 years old.

This account is funded by the parents and can only be used for college. If the money is used for anything else, you will have to pay penalties. The money can also be used for another child or relative if the one for who it was intended didn't use it.

There are income limits. For example, if you (the parents) make more than $95,000-$110,000 for single persons or $190,000 - $220,000 for married couples, you can't contribute to the ESA. However, you can give the money to your child and he/she can open the account him/herself.

The money can also be used to fund K-12 education and/or supplies.

TRICKY TITLES

The *Coverdell Education Savings Account* (ESA) was also known as an *Education IRA*, before people realized that the ESA isn't for retirement.

An ESA account is a great choice for kids who don't yet earn an income, but still want to save money for college.

POP QUIZ

1. When do you have to pay taxes on a ROTH IRA?
a. When you withdraw the money
b. When you visit the money
c. When you deposit the money
d. When you paint the money

2. Do you have to pay penalties if you took the money out of a Traditional IRA account on your 32nd birthday?
a. Nope, the money's yours after all
b. Yes, definitely, the money is only for retirement
c. Only if you can sing.

3. What does ESA stand for?
a. Education Savings Account
b. Elephants Sitting Around
c. Egg Shell Association
d. Energetic Snakes Accounting

4. Which retirement account requires you to withdraw your money by age 701/2?
a. Traditional IRA
b. ESA
c. ROTH IRA
d. WSA

5. What does tax-deductible mean?
a. Money deposited into the account is taxed
b. You get $100 on Tax Day
c. The money is used to buy every person a German shepherd
d. Money deposited into the account isn't taxed.

Answers: 1.C 2.B 3.A 4.A 5.D

Chapter 10

An Employer Plan

The types of accounts that we discussed in the last chapter are types of **individual** retirement accounts. These are accounts that you set up and manage yourself. An **employer plan** is an account that you can set up through your employer. The benefit of this is that the contributions are deducted *automatically* from your paycheck, without you having to do a thing.

This type of account is known as an employer plan, or more commonly as a 401k/403b plan. These employer plans are for employees who work for a company that doesn't offer pension plans. **Pension plans** are a small salary that the company pays out to you when you retire as a reward for working at their company. Some companies offer matching contributions to incentivize you to put money in the plan.

TAKING NOTE

A 403B plan is for employees who work for a non-profit organization such as schools and hospitals.

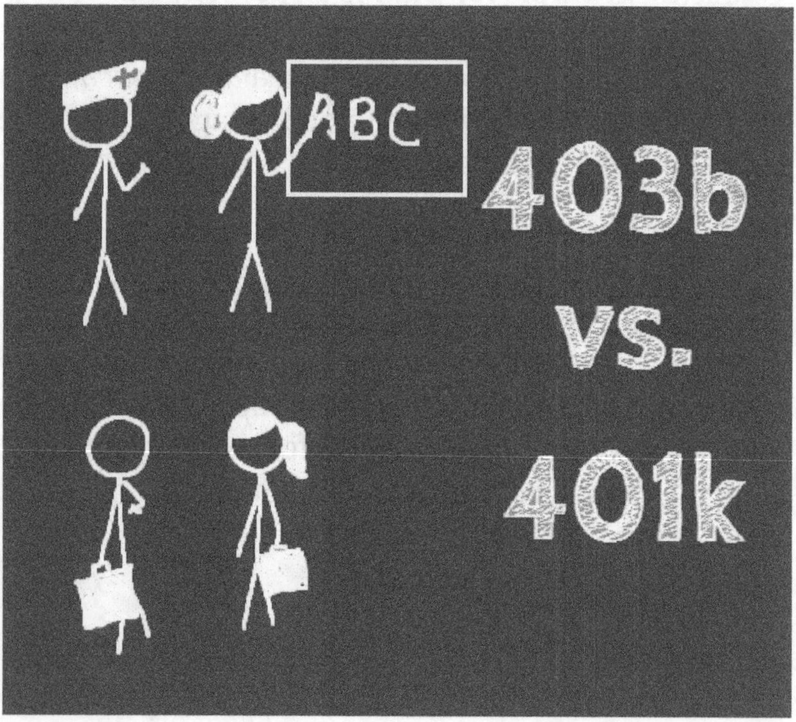

Benefits of setting up an employer plan include:

- You do not pay income tax on money put into the plan
- You do not pay income tax on the returns gained
- Only pay when you withdraw your money
- Maximum yearly contribution: $17,500
- Maximum yearly contribution if over 50: $23,000
- Can make contributions automatic through payroll deduction (taking money from your paycheck)
- Some companies offer to match your contributions, which is FREE MONEY

NAUGHTY NUMBERS

The numbers and letters in 401k and 403b refer to the part of the tax code that established these retirement plans.

Many big companies choose to match up to 50 cents on the dollar of what you contribute. What this means is, if you make $100,000 a year, and you put 10% of that money, or $10,000 into a 401k, the company will give you an additional 5% to put into your account, or half of what you contributed. Total, you will have 15%.

A 401k is similar to a Traditional IRA, in that you only pay taxes when you withdraw the money. The main difference is that the plan is set up through your employer.

The biggest benefit of the 401k/403b plan is that you can contribute a much larger maximum amount than with an IRA. The second benefit is of matching contributions. Take advantage of this opportunity and contribute at least a percentage of your salary, if not more. This is free money!

POP QUIZ

1. What is a 401(k)?
a. 401 year kangaroos
b. An employer plan
c. A party planner
d. Taxes

2. What is a matching contribution?
a. Donations to charity
b. A card game
c. Free money
d. Give a man a fish

3. Do you manage a 401k/403b like an IRA?
a. No, a 401k/403b is set up through your employer

b. No, it's managed by a professionally hired team of trapeze artists
c. Yes, I manage everything myself
d. Yes, a 401k is an IRA

4. What is a 403b plan for?
a. Artists
b. Lawyers
c. Politicians (there always has to be a politician)
d. Non-profit organizations

5. What is the maximum amount of money you can contribute to a 401k/403b plan each year if you're under 50?
a. $2,000
b. $23,000
c. $17,500
d. $175,000

Answers: 1.B 2.C 3.A 4.D 5.C

Chapter 11

Setting up an Account

Now that you know the different kinds of retirement accounts, it's time to take the next step in your journey. It is time for you to finally set up your retirement or brokerage account! Sound scary? Don't worry, we've got you covered.

A retirement account is devoted to retirement; most accounts that you personally handle will be an IRA. To set up a 401(k), talk to your employer. Brokerage accounts aren't specific to retirement; they simply allow you to buy and sell stocks or bonds in an account, but it is not put towards retirement.

If you are a minor, you can open a **guardian account**. The account is opened in the parent's name and owned by the parent. The funds, or money is taxed at the parent's rate. Once you turn 18, ownership of the funds is turned over to you. Another option is a **custodial account**; the parent controls the account, but you own it. The funds are taxed at the child rate rather than the parent's. Once you turn 18, you are allowed to control the funds as well as own it.

Most of the time, you set up a retirement account with a brokerage firm. Brokerage firms handle both retirement and brokerage accounts. Many brokerage firms have an online website that makes it easy to set up and manage your account. Some have brick and mortar branch offices where you can come and talk to people face-to-face.

Many also have phone support and people that can guide you through the process of setting up your retirement account. Ready to click that button or make that call? Here is a list of brokerage firms that make it easy to set up a retirement or brokerage account:

	MINIMUM AMOUNT	COMMISSION SCHEDULE	IRA FEES
TD Ameritrade	Retirement (IRA) No Minimum	Online Stock Trades $9.99 Touchtone Phone Trades $34.99 Broker Assisted Trades $44.99	Maintenance None Account Transfer Out $25.00 Wire Out Fees $15.00 Certificate Fee $40.00
Share Builder	Retirement (IRA) No Minimum	Automatic Investments As low as $1.00 Real-time Investments $6.95	Maintenance None Account Transfer Out $15-$75

Fidelity Investments	Retirement (IRA) $2,500	Online Stock Trades As low as $7.95 Touchtone Phone Trades As low as $12.95 Broker Assisted Trades As low as $32.95	Maintenance None Account Transfer Out $50 Wire Out Fees Fed wires may apply
Charles Schwab	Retirement (IRA) $1,000	Online Stock Trades $8.95 Touchtone Phone Trades $13.95 Broker Assisted Trades $33.95	Maintenance $0 Account Transfer-Partial $25 Account Transfer-Full $50

Vanguard	Retirement (IRA) $1,000	Online Stock Trades Vanguard ETFs trade commission-free Stocks and non-Vanguard ETFs $7 for first 25 trades, $20 for subsequent trades	Account Transfer Out $0 Wire Out Fees $0 Maintenance $20 annual fee for brokerage + mutual fund accounts
Scottrade Inc.	Retirement (IRA) $500	Online Stock Trades $7.00 Touchtone Phone Trades $17.00 Broker Assisted Trades	Maintenance None Account Transfer Out $75 Wire Out Fees $25-$40

The fees for stock trades apply only to market and limit orders. For special orders, other fees may apply. Be sure to check your broker's website for more information.

The lowest trade cost applies when you do your transaction through a computer. Touchtone Phone trades are when you call your brokerage firm and there is a system in place that allows you to manage your account or buy and sell stocks. The transaction is done over the phone, but without a broker. Finally, broker-assisted trades are where a broker assists you and places your transaction. These typically cost more because you have to pay for the broker's services.

IRA Maintenance fees pay for the services that your brokers provide by submitting certain information to the IRS (Internal Revenue Service). However, most brokerages don't charge maintenance fees anymore.

The transfer fees are for when you're transferring the money in your account to another brokerage firm.

Wire-out fees apply when transferring money to other banks or countries.

RETIREMENT QUIZ

1. What are the four types of accounts you learned?
a. ROTH, IRA, ESA, 401k/403b
b. THOR, ARI, ASE, k104/b304
c. HATH, SCUBA, TTLY, UR
d. Savings, Money, TIMER, WTR

2. At what age are you fully responsible for your money?
a. 16
b. 0
c. 70 ½
d. 18

3. When can you open an IRA account?
a. Anytime
b. After you turn 18
c. Once you earn an annual income
d. When you've lived through a whole century

Answers: 1.A 2.D 3.C

Worksheets

Here are some extra blank charts to fill out and assist you in your journey.

Goal Setting Chart:

Date	Goal	How You Will Achieve Your Goal	Estimated Cost	Deadline Date	Achieved (Y or N)

The Habitual Factor Chart:

	ITEMS BOUGHT						$ SPENT DAILY
MON.	Item: Price:	Item: Price:	Item: Price:	Item: Price:	Item: Price:	Item: Price:	
TUES.	Item: Price:	Item: Price:	Item: Price:	Item: Price:	Item: Price:	Item: Price:	
WED.	Item: Price:	Item: Price:	Item: Price:	Item: Price:	Item: Price:	Item: Price:	
THUR.	Item: Price:	Item: Price:	Item: Price:	Item: Price:	Item: Price:	Item: Price:	
FRI.	Item: Price:	Item: Price:	Item: Price:	Item: Price:	Item: Price:	Item: Price:	
SAT.	Item: Price:	Item: Price:	Item: Price:	Item: Price:	Item: Price:	Item: Price:	
SUN.	Item: Price:	Item: Price:	Item: Price:	Item: Price:	Item: Price:	Item: Price:	
GRAND TOTAL							

Cash Inflow Chart

Date	Money From:	Amount	Running Total

Cash Gift Chart

Free to Spend 10%	Cost
Saved 80%	
- Bonds	
- Savings Account	
- Retirement Account	
- Stocks	
- Commodities	
Charity 10%	
- Local Charities	
- National / Intl. Charities	
- KIVA (invest in people)	
Total:	

Bond Buying Tracking Chart:

	ISSUER	TYPE	MATURITY DATE	PAR	YIELD	TERM	RATING
1							
2							
3							
4							
5							
6							
7							
8							
9							
10							
11							
12							
13							
14							
15							

Stock Research Chart:

	Sector	Stock	Symbol	Exchange	Price	Dividend	P/E
1							
2							
3							
4							
5							
6							
7							
8							
9							
10							
11							
12							
13							

Stock Holdings Tracker:

	Ticker Symbol	Action	Price	Number of Shares	Total Invested
1					
2					
3					
4					
5					
6					
7					
8					
9					
10					
11					
12					
13					
14					
15					

Monitor Your Portfolio

Date	Balance	Investment	Cost	Money Received	New Balance

Bibliography

BOOKS:

- *Real Money: Sane Investing in an Insane World,* by Jim Cramer
- *The Automatic Millionaire* by David Bach
- *Million Dollar Portfolio,* by David and Tom Gardner
- *Action Plan*, by Suze Orman
- *The Money Book for the Young, Fabulous and Broke*, by Suze Orman
- *The Millionaire Next Door*, by Thomas Stanley and William Danko
- *The Secrets of the Millionaire Mind*, by T. Eker
- *How to Get Wfhat You Want*, by Zig Ziglar
- *The Motley Fool's Investment Guide for Teens* by David and Tom Gardner
- *Barron's Dictionary of Finance and Investment Terms* – Eighth Edition by John Downes, A.B. and Jordan Elliot Goodman, A.B., M.A.

WEBSITES:

- www.finance.yahoo.com/
- www.cnbc.com/
- www.thestreet.com/
- www.nasdaq.com/
- www.investopedia.com/
- www.fool.com/
- www.irs.com/
- nyse.nyx.com/
- Finance section on www.about.com/

Glossary

401(k) / 403(b) – see employer plan

annuity – a form of contract sold by life insurance companies that guarantees a fixed or variable payment to the annuitant at some future time, usually retirement.

ask / asked price – the price at which a security or commodity is offered for sale on an exchange or in the over-the-counter market. Generally, it is the lowest round lot price at which a dealer will sell.

bid – price a prospective buyer is ready to pay.

bond - any interest-bearing or discounted government or corporate security that obligates the issuer to pay the bondholder a specified sum of money, and to repay the principal amount of the loan at maturity.

compound interest - interest earned on principal plus interest that was earned earlier.

corporate bond - debt instrument issued by a private corporation, as distinct from one issued by a government agency or a municipality.

coupon rate – see yield

credit card - a small plastic card issued by a bank, business, etc., allowing the holder to purchase goods or services on credit.

debit card - a card issued by a bank allowing the holder to transfer money electronically to another bank account when making a purchase.

debt - something, typically money, that is owed or due.

deducted - subtract or take away (an amount or part) from a total.

earned income - money derived from paid work.

employer plan - a highly regulated and restricted tax-qualified retirement plan that an employer establishes to benefit employees.

EPS / Earnings Per Share – a portion of a company's profit allocated to each outstanding share of common stock

ESA / Coverdell Education Savings Account – an account created to encourage parents to save for their children's education

expense ratio - a measure of what it costs an investment company to operate a mutual fund

face value -the nominal value or dollar value of a security stated by the issuer. For stocks, it is the original cost of the stock shown on the certificate.

For bonds, it is the amount paid to the holder at maturity (generally $1,000). Also known as "par value" or simply "par."

HECM / Home Equity Conversion Mortgage (Reverse Mortgage) - a reverse mortgage (or lifetime mortgage) is a loan available to seniors, and is used to release the home equity in the property as one lump sum or multiple payments. The homeowner's obligation to repay the loan is deferred until the owner dies, the home is sold, or the owner leaves

income - money received, esp. on a regular basis, for work or through investments.

income tax - tax levied by a government directly on income, esp. an annual tax on personal income

ETF / Exchange Traded Fund - a mutual fund that is traded on a stock exchange.

inflation - a general increase in prices and fall in the purchasing value of money.

interest - the charge for the privilege of borrowing money, typically expressed as an annual percentage rate.

IPO / Initial Public Offering - the first sale of stock by a private company to the public.

IRA / Individual Retirement Account - an investing tool used by individuals to earn and earmark funds for retirement savings.

issuer - a legal entity that develops, registers and sells securities for the purpose of financing its operations.

limit order - an order placed with a brokerage to buy or sell a set number of shares at a specified price or better.

market order - an order that an investor makes through a broker or brokerage service to buy or sell an investment immediately at the best available current price.

maturity date - the date on which the principal amount of a note, draft, acceptance bond or other debt instrument becomes due and is repaid to the investor and interest payments stop.

municipal bond - debt obligation of a state or local government entity. The funds may support general governmental needs or special projects.

mutual fund - an investment program funded by shareholders that trades in diversified holdings and is professionally managed.

par – see face value

payroll deduction - amount withheld by an employer from employee's earnings.

penalty (retirement) - a special additional tax of 10% due if one takes a distribution from their retirement plans (such as a 401(k) or IRA prior to reaching age 59 ½ or meeting some exception.

pension plan - a type of retirement plan, usually tax exempt, wherein an employer makes contributions toward a pool of funds set aside for an employee's future benefit. The pool of funds is then invested on the employee's behalf, allowing the employee to receive benefits upon retirement.

principle - the original amount invested, separate from earnings or the face value of a bond.

profit - a financial gain, esp. the difference between the amount earned and the amount spent in buying, operating, producing or investing in something.

retirement account - a plan for setting aside money to be spent after retirement.

risk - The chance that an investment's actual return will be different than expected. Risk includes the possibility of losing some or all of the original investment.

ROTH IRA - an individual retirement account allowing a person to set aside after-tax income up to a specified amount each year. Both earnings on the account and withdrawals after age 59½ are tax-free.

savings bond - a bond issued by the government and sold to the general public.

sector - An industry or market sharing common characteristics.

share - one of the equal parts into which a company's capital is divided, entitling the holder to a proportion of the profits. (a share of a company)

simple interest - interest calculation based only on the original principle amount.

spread - the difference between the bid and the ask price of a security or asset.

stock - ownership of a corporation represented by shares that are a claim on the corporation's earnings and assets.

term - a fixed or limited period for which an investment, lasts or is intended to last.

ticker symbol - a stock symbol or ticker symbol is a short abbreviation used to uniquely identify publicly traded shares of a particular stock on a particular stock market.

Traditional IRA - an individual retirement account (IRA) that allows individuals to direct pretax income, up to specific annual limits, toward investments that can grow tax-deferred (no capital gains or dividend income is taxed)

Treasury Bond - . a government bond issued by the US Treasury.

unearned income - income from investments rather than from work.

yield - the income return on an investment. This refers to the interest or dividends received from a security and is usually expressed annually as a percentage based on the investment's cost, its current market value or its face value.

ABOUT THE AUTHOR/ ILLUSTRATOR

Diana spent the first part of her childhood in Florida where she was born in 1999 and currently lives in the Seattle area. She lives with her three younger sisters and her parents. She loves her family, friends, tennis, piano and programming. Her curiosity for how the world works inspired her to decrypt the world of finance. She wishes that everyone can learn how to save and invest their money early on so that people can achieve financial freedom and live with dignity.

Connect with the author at: dianabank99@gmail.com

www.ingramcontent.com/pod-product-compliance
Lightning Source LLC
Chambersburg PA
CBHW051214170526
45166CB00005B/1890
* 9 7 8 1 4 9 3 5 1 5 4 5 5 *